Looking
after your

Expert advice from:

Kristina Routh, MBChB, MPH
Medical Consultant

Bethany Florey MSc
Registered Dietitian

Dr Angharad Rudkin
Clinical Psychologist, University of Southampton

USBORNE

Looking
after your
Health

Caroline Young

Designed by
Stephanie Jeffries

Illustrated by
Freya Harrison, Nancy Leschnikoff
and Christyan Fox

Edited by
Felicity Brooks

Usborne Quicklinks

The internet is a great source of information, but it's very important to know which sites you can trust.

We have selected some useful websites to supplement the information in this book and these are available at **Usborne Quicklinks**. Here you can find helpful tips on healthy eating, and learn more about topics such as mindfulness.

For links to all these sites, go to:
usborne.com/Quicklinks
and type in the title of this book.

Please follow the internet safety guidelines at Usborne Quicklinks. Children should be supervised online.

Introduction

Your health is probably the most important thing you'll ever have, but how much time do you spend looking after it? If your honest answer is 'not much', then **this book is for you.** It's full of facts, tips and advice to help you live healthily without a) joining an expensive gym; b) feeling hungry 24/7 or c) having a personality transplant.

You'll find chapters about how to eat well, build up your exercise level, sleep better and cope with stress. There's information about your mental health, too, because being truly healthy includes being happy.

Remember, your health has to last **your whole life,** so try to take good care of it <u>NOW</u>...

Contents

Chapter 1

So, what is health?

How are you feeling? Bursting with energy and raring to go, or a bit fed-up, and wishing you were lying on a beach? Well, to be honest, none of us can possibly look or feel fabulous all the time (whatever your social media feed might tell you) but one of the best things you can do to make sure you feel as good as you possibly can is to look after your health. So, read on...

'Health' is a massive subject, so let's start with what the word means to you. Does it make you think of eating piles of cabbage, running a marathon or sprinkling everything you eat with seeds? (Though all these things are great, if they make you feel good.)

I want to be more healthy, but how?

If you really aren't sure about what's healthy and what's not, **don't worry**: this book will tell you all you need to know and give you plenty of everyday ideas and tips to help you. Living healthily is an amazingly positive thing: it means being able to **live your best life,** and taking the very best care of yourself. Your health really is the most important thing you will ever have, so it's worth looking after. It's time to find out how...

What makes us healthy?

Being healthy is much more than not being ill.

Put very simply, how healthy you are depends on:

WHAT YOU **EAT** **WHAT YOU** **HOW YOU** **FEEL** **DO**

Of course, many other things play a part and some of them (such as not always being able to make your own choices about what you eat at home) may be tricky to change. BUT there are lots of things that you CAN do to make sure you live as healthily as you can. You could try out some of the ideas in this book and see which ones you like. You might find making changes easier than you thought.

Quick quiz

Right, let's start by seeing how you
answer these four simple questions.
Be **honest**, please.

1. **If you're hungry, what's your go-to snack?**
a) An apple
b) A packet of crisps or chocolate bar
c) A bowl of cereal

2. **When you finish school, what do you like to do?**
a) Play football or go for a walk
b) Watch TV or go online until dinner
c) Play computer games

3. **What would you rather eat, given the choice?**
a) A crisp, fresh salad and baked potato
b) Chips and curry sauce
c) A pizza, with loads of different toppings

4. Choose one of these words to best describe how you feel right now:

a) Happy
b) Hopeful
c) Tired

TRICK OR TRUTH?

Sorry, but that was a bit of a trick quiz. Whichever answers you chose, none of them is 'wrong'. Sometimes crisps or a pizza are exactly what you want, and sometimes you'll feel tired. That's life. What's important is to remember that being healthy is about getting the **balance** right, rather than never being able to eat, do or feel certain things. Phew!

One and only

The human body is truly amazing, whatever shape, size, age or colour it may be. You can find out more about which bit inside your body does what, and why you need to take care of all these bits, in the next chapter. You'll also see just how incredible we all are.

It's really worth remembering, when you think about your body, that **you only get <u>ONE</u>** – designed to last for your whole life – so the choices you make, and the habits you form when you're young, can make a real difference. Making good, healthy choices now means you will take care of that one-and-only body of yours as well as you can.

Taking care of my body is a great idea!

Good... and bad

Luckily, you've picked a pretty good time to be alive, all things considered. In the past, life was much tougher. It's easier to stay happy and healthy now than it has ever been, for these main reasons:

Just be glad you didn't live when I did.

- Most people don't get eaten by wild animals (as some did in the past).
- Scientists have found treatments for lots of horrible diseases.
- Many of us have a huge choice of food.
- Many of us have lots more free time.

These, and some other factors, mean that many people now live for longer than they have ever done,

BUT (and it's a big 'but')...

...we face health problems today that many people didn't face in the past. Here are the main ones:

- Our lifestyles are causing new health problems, such as obesity.
- A HUGE choice of food can mean we don't always choose healthily and makes it easy to eat too much.
- Not everyone can easily buy and cook healthy food.
- Many people have too much stress in their lives, and are unhappy.
- A lot of us are always tired, because we don't get enough sleep.

Doesn't sound great, does it? Living a long life is fab, if what you do with it keeps you healthy and happy, but lots of people are missing out. Let's whizz through these modern health problems, and see how they may affect young people in particular.

What is obesity?

Health experts are worried because more and more people are unhealthily overweight, or 'obese'. They believe that there are two main reasons for this:

- We sit in cars, or at desks, instead of walking or doing physical work (as people did in the past).
- We eat too much – especially unhealthy food. End of.

So we are less active than we used to be, but we eat lots more, so we put on weight. This can also lead to an illness called diabetes, which is a particularly worrying trend among young people. **Not good.**

Too much choice?

In the past, many people were more worried about not getting enough food to eat than what they fancied for tea. Today, we tend to eat big portions and snack too often, and supermarkets are crammed with thousands of different kinds of food. Snacks and chocolate are carefully displayed and branded to tempt shoppers to pop them into the trolley – especially children and young people. If you just want a drink, there are dozens to choose from...

What is stress?

Stress, put simply, is when our bodies find it too difficult to cope with what's going on around us, so are on 'high alert', making us feel as if we're in danger, all the time. It's absolutely exhausting.

This really affects our mental health and many young people feel stressed by all the pressures around them. In the past, people probably didn't realize that they were stressed as there were too many other things to worry about — like surviving.

The cost of food

Research has found that, in some places, healthy
food is too expensive for a lot of people, or tricky
to buy. In some areas, there are more takeaways
and fast food outlets than food shops or markets,
which makes healthy eating hard. Busy young
people can easily get into the habit of eating
unhealthily, or 'on the go', and more parents work
than in the past, so don't have time to cook as
much at home. All this can lead to basic cooking
skills getting lost.

Free time

Before TV and computers were invented (not THAT long ago!) young people played sports, walked home, did chores or played games after sitting down for most of the day at school. If you still do these things, that's great, but experts worry that too many young people are now spending long hours playing computer games, or glued to a screen – often on their own. Not only is this a bit lonely, but it involves even more sitting down (and probably snacking at the same time. Oops!).

Sleep

Sleep is especially important for young people, as their bodies and minds need rest to be happy and healthy. In the past, most people went to bed early and got up early (well, there was no electric light, and no TV, of course). Today, experts think that too many young people are on their phones, tablets, laptops or games consoles when they should be sleeping. This can leave them 'sleep deprived' if it goes on too long, which is not good at all.

As you can see, there's **lots** to think about, but **don't worry**. There are ways of tackling these problems, and you'll find out how in this book. Once you know, you'll never look back.

Chapter 2

Your amazing body

A healthy body is something people often take for granted... until something goes wrong with it, and they feel ill. Let's take a look inside, to see what's keeping you alive and well.

Every single thing
inside your body has a job to do...
and there are **thousands**
of things in there!

Medical experts group all the things inside our bodies into eleven different systems*, but five organs (let's call them **The Fab Five**) are <u>absolutely essential</u>.

* Go to Usborne Quicklinks (see page 4) to find out more about these systems.

If any one of The Fab Five stops working properly, we can become very ill indeed, and sometimes die. Sadly, illness can strike any of us at any time, but how we live our lives, what we eat and drink, and how active we are, really affects the health of these five life-giving organs. It's worth giving them the best possible chance then, isn't it?

THE FAB FIVE

1 HEART

When your heart beats, it pumps blood around your body. It beats about 100,000 times a day, 24/7, for the whole of your life.

2 BRAIN

Your brain is the control hub of your body. It's thinking, feeling and sending messages to other parts of your body every single minute of every day.

3 KIDNEYS

Your (two) kidneys help filter your blood, and create urine (wee). All the blood in your body will pass through your kidneys many times a day.

4 LIVER

Your liver removes toxins from your blood, and doesn't work as well if you're overweight. (But luckily for us, it can usually repair itself if it's not in tip-top condition. Hooray!)

5 LUNGS

Your lungs take in oxygen as you breathe in, and get rid of carbon dioxide as you breathe out. Your left lung is a bit smaller, to fit your heart in your chest, but they both work very hard.

Yeah, if I had to pick 5, these would be my faves.

As well as The Fab Five, thousands of other things help your body to function well, including...

- Your **stomach**, which has muscles that pummel your food for about 3 hours before it goes into your intestines (guts).

- Your **small and large intestines** process your food. Put together, they'd probably stretch all the way around your bed. Nice.

- Your **bladder** stores urine (wee). It can hold up to a litre (1 ¾ pints), but you'll probably feel the need to go when it's only a quarter full.

- Your **skin** covers and protects your body, and is constantly renewing itself. So... protect your great protector by always wearing a hat and sunscreen on sunny days.

And here's one last fact to amaze you:

- You have enough **blood vessels** in your body to stretch around the world – TWICE!

Illness

This book is all about healthy living and being well, but, from time to time, most of us fall ill. It's **normal,** and part of being alive, so let's talk a bit about being unwell, too.

It's true that all the things you'll read about in this book (exercising regularly, having a balanced diet and trying to be kind to yourself amidst the pressures of life) are vital parts of the 'staying healthy' recipe. Living healthily will really help your body fend off many bugs and sniffles.

But there are no guarantees. Illness
happens to all of us at some
point in our lives,
whatever we do,
eat or feel.

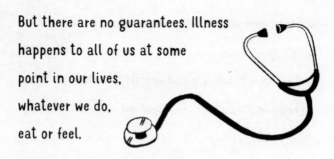

There are many kinds of illness and they vary in
their symptoms and their seriousness. Vaccines
and immunisation can stop people getting some
of the most serious illnesses, such as cholera and
polio, but some incurable diseases remain. Luckily,
research is going on all the time to find cures for
them, too. Yay!

So the good news is that many dangerous illnesses are now curable. The not-so-good news is that new diseases emerge from time to time. The Coronavirus (COVID-19) is one of these, and scientists are working very hard to find a vaccine for it. As a general rule with any cold or flu-like symptoms: <u>wash your hands</u> frequently, <u>use tissues</u> when you sneeze, and <u>cover your mouth</u> when you cough. Do all you can to avoid passing your germs on.

Despite all the medicines, research and treatment, you may know someone in your family, or friendship circle, who has been affected by a serious illness. If you do, and it upsets or worries you, **talk to someone about it.** Although illness is the 'dark side' of health, it needs to be discussed, especially when sad things happen to someone you care about.

Common illnesses

On the bright side, thankfully, most young people only experience what are known

as 'minor illnesses'. These might include tummy bugs, a headache or a fever. Most school days are missed due to colds, sore throats, coughs, or flu (a horrible combo of all three) which is grim. These illnesses do go, but you may need to rest, drink plenty of water and take painkillers until they do.

All about antibiotics

Antibiotics are drugs that can cure illnesses caused by bacteria. They have saved millions of lives, but can stop working if people take them too often, or if they're taken for illnesses they can't cure, such as colds and most sore throats (which are caused by viruses).

Unfortunately, some conditions often affect young people in particular:

- **Asthma** in which people struggle to breathe during an attack. This is made worse by air pollution, a concern in busy cities. It's usually treated with medication, which is breathed-in through an inhaler.

- **Eczema** in which the skin itches, flakes and cracks, and gets terribly sore. This can make life very difficult, and many experts believe it's linked to stress. This, too, can usually be managed by medication.

- **Epilepsy** in which people have 'seizures' (that used to be called 'fits') is a serious illness. It's caused by lots of electrical messages 'misfiring' in the brain, but is usually treatable with medication and sometimes a special diet.

Things you can't see

Sometimes, the way some people behave can be mistaken for illnesses, but it's actually because their brains work in slightly different ways. These differences are known as 'neurological diversity'. Here are four you may recognize but there are many more:

Dyslexia
problems reading letters

Dyspraxia
problems with bodily co-ordination

ADHD (Attention Deficit Hyperactivity Disorder)
in which people struggle to concentrate and are likely to act impulsively, amongst other things

Autism
problems communicating and relating to others in daily life

Today, many more people are diagnosed as being autistic, or 'on the autistic spectrum'. Nobody knows what causes autism, but for years it was misdiagnosed. It's good to know something about it.

Someone who is autistic sees the world differently, and they can find things that most of us do every day really tricky. Lots of noise, a big social gathering, making decisions and being rushed can be especially stressful for them: school is often a particularly difficult environment for someone who is autistic.

If you know someone who is on the autistic spectrum, or different in any other way, **be patient and kind.** There are many ways of being human, and we <u>all</u> deserve kindness, don't we?

Body image

While we're talking about our bodies, there's another problem that young people face more today than ever before. There's huge pressure to have The Perfect Body, and this impossible goal is having a huge impact on how many young people feel about themselves. Feeling inadequate about yourself in comparison to others is not healthy, and can lead to real problems. Social media, and the people that use it as a platform to make themselves famous, have had a big part to play in stoking this problem. Striving for perfection like this, and worrying because you can't achieve it (well, who can?) is really bad for your mental health.

There's more about this important issue coming up, but try taking this quiz, just to get an idea of how you feel about your body (called your body image):

Quick quiz

1. Do you enjoy trying on clothes in shop changing rooms?
   a) No, I hate it. I always try things on at home.
   b) Yeah, it's fun, even if I look awful in them.
   c) If I'm feeling confident, yes, but sometimes, no.

2. If you go swimming, do you mind showing more of your body?
   a) I hate it. People see the bits I want to hide.
   b) Bring it on!
   c) There are bits of me I don't like, but who doesn't feel like that?

3. Looking at other people, what do you see?
   a) Everyone else is so much better-looking than me.
   b) I see people, in all shapes and sizes. End of.
   c) Sometimes I wish I looked different, but usually I am happy with who I am.

Answers

If you chose mainly a) answers, you don't seem too happy in your own skin, but there's no need to worry. Read the rest of this book, and hopefully, you'll change your mind.

If you went for the b) answers, you have a positive body image. Good for you: you're rare!

If you chose the c) answers, you're probably like almost everyone you meet: you like some things about your body, but not everything, all the time. All quite normal, folks.

Real or fake?

So, it's clear that 'perfectionism' (or the quest to be perfect) is an important mental health issue right now. If it affects you, or someone you know, it might help to remember that so many of the photos you see on social media, or in celebrity magazines, are the result of hours and hours spent getting the person in the pictures made-up, groomed and dressed. Then even more hours are spent altering the pictures digitally to remove every spot, cellulite dimple or dark shadow and to create bulging biceps or a six-pack. In fact, many celebrities say that they dread going outside and being seen as they really are because this is so different to the image the public usually see. That's pretty sad, isn't it?

If you compare yourself with these altered images, you're heading for a whole lot of disappointment and frustration, so try as hard as you can not to, and to see them for what they are – **fake**. It's a much healthier approach.

 I wish I had luscious lips, or a HUUUGE bum.

I wish I had a six-pack. Or even a two-pack!

 I think you're both great just as you are.

If you use filters on your selfies, that's fun, as long as you don't feel you should actually look like that filtered photo, or that other people will expect you to.

Be happy with yourself as you are!

If you have a few spots, fine.
There are ways of tackling
them on page 105. If you'd like
to be a bit slimmer, check out
the healthy recipes on pages

189 to 197. If you wish you were fitter,
or more ripped, check out the ideas in **Chapter 6**.
Yep, this book is full of ways to make yourself
even more wonderful than you already are.

Self-image

How you feel about yourself as a whole, as a person, is called your self-image. Sorry to break it to you, but it can be seriously affected by going on that elusive 'quest for perfection'. It can really undermine how you see yourself in the world, too.

There's more about how all this can affect your mental health in **Chapters 7** and **8**, but for now, let's take a closer look at this whole self-image thing.

Do you feel good?

Well... do you? Read this:

I like myself.

Now try saying it out loud. That's probably really hard, isn't it? We all tend to think of what's wrong with us, rather than what's right. Now, answer these questions as **honestly** as you can:

1. Do you find it difficult to look in a mirror?
2. Do you often compare yourself to other people?
3. Would you change a lot about yourself, if you could?
4. Have you ever avoided a social gathering because you feel you don't look good?
5. Do you ever wish you were a different person altogether?

Well, as you've probably guessed, if you answered **'Yes'** to more than one of these questions, your self-image might not be the best. This is very common, but it's also very sad, because you are a <u>unique and fabulous</u> person (yay!). You just need to **believe it.** Read on...

I am fab!

Positive statements like that, and the one on page 40, are called affirmations and you may find it a bit difficult and embarrassing to say them at first, but if you keep repeating them, either out loud, or in your head, they can make a real difference. Find somewhere you won't be disturbed. Then, choose one of these statements and say it right now:

I am so much more than how I look.

♥

I love and respect my amazing body just as it is.

♥

Nobody has the right to judge me on my appearance.

♥

I am not an object to be looked at. I am a person.

♥

I am just as good as anyone else
in this world.

OK, there may well be things you want to change about yourself. Just about everyone feels like that at times, but it's best to focus on the things you can change (your hairstyle, your 'look', your hobbies) and give them your best shot. Then you can try to accept the things you can't (your height, your family, your deep love of gherkins). Obsessing about negative stuff will get you nowhere fast.

Accepting yourself, and having a positive self-image takes time and practice as the pressure to be perfect is so strong. But it's worth it, and will stand you in good stead for the rest of your life.

And here's one final fact for you:

NOBODY
IS PERFECT.

Chapter 3

Let's talk about food

Everyone needs food. It helps your body grow and repair itself, fends off illness and basically makes sure all the things that need to happen keep on happening! It's good to eat healthily, but there's no one way of doing it. Here are some of the food choices people make:

I eat EVERYTHING.

I eat fish, but not meat.

I don't eat meat or fish.

I eat a plant-based diet.

I only eat organic food.

I don't eat dairy.

Having said that there's a lot of choice, as a young person, you may not feel that this is true. You probably don't make all your own meals, so you might feel you don't have much say in what you eat. That's understandable, but **you <u>can</u> change it,** and have more control – especially if you know what kinds of food it's best to eat. You may well find that the adults doing the shopping and cooking in your household are glad of your help, and might let you cook meals for your family from time to time. **Go you!**

What's for lunch?

I don't know. You tell me!

Food as fuel

Your body is growing and changing very rapidly during your teenage years and what you eat is very important. Just as an engine needs the right fuel, your body needs good food to run well. Here are five types of food to choose from:

1. CARBS (or CARBOHYDRATES)
bread, potatoes, rice, pasta and cereals (grains)

These foods give us energy, so you really need them. They are called 'starchy carbohydrates' (which doesn't sound good, but actually is – very).

2. FRUIT & VEG
fruit and vegetables, really, like it says
(fresh, frozen or canned)

The foods in this group are vital for staying healthy. You should aim to eat at least five portions of them a day (but a portion is only one apple, a satsuma or two carrots).

3. PROTEIN
meat, fish, eggs, nuts, beans, lentils

These foods are full of protein, which strengthens muscles, builds strong bones, and helps our bodies heal. Good stuff, really.

4. DAIRY
milk, cheese, yogurt

These all contain calcium, which you need for strong bones, muscles and good teeth. You don't need too much of them though and it's best to choose some lower fat versions.

Eat some kind of calcium-rich food with each meal if you can.

5. FAT & SUGAR
cakes, biscuits, sweets, crisps and snacks

Most of us like cakes, biscuits, chocolate and crisps, but try not to eat too many of the foods in this group. They are fab as treats but don't help your body to work well. #sadbuttruefact

A guide to eating well

To eat healthily, you need a variety of foods. This chart, called The Eatwell Guide, shows the recommended proportions of each type. You'll see you need to aim for more of some than of others.

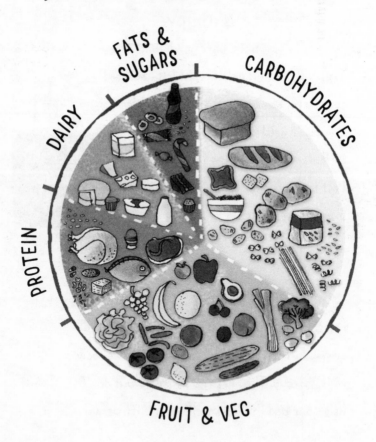

FATS & SUGARS

CARBOHYDRATES

DAIRY

PROTEIN

FRUIT & VEG

So, it's more veg for me, then.

Of course, you can't measure absolutely everything you eat, but you can clearly see what you need to eat more of to stay healthy, can't you? From now on, aim to eat most of your food from these sections:

CARBOHYDRATES

PROTEIN   FRUIT & VEG

You can eat the things in the 'Dairy' and 'Fats & sugars' sections... just not too much of them, OK?

A closer look

Now for more detail and tips for including a balance of these five groups of food in your daily diet. You'll find lots more recipes, suggestions and general foody tips in the 'Health for life' section on pages 185 to 197.

> I need food right NOW!

Starchy carbohydrates

These foods are fabulous fuel for your body and should make up about a third of all the food you eat. Carbs are absolutely vital, because when you eat them, they provide your body with the energy it needs, but you can make them really healthy by trying the tips coming up next...

TOP TIPS

- Swap white bread for healthier wholemeal, seeded or 'half and half' bread.
- Try wholemeal (brown) pasta, brown rice, or wild rice from time to time.
- Instead of having chips, make some spicy sweet potato wedges (see the recipe on page 189).
- Think about portion size. About a third of your plate should be carbs — but no more.

After that super-healthy breakfast, I could bounce all day!

Fruit and vegetables

These foods are full of vitamins and minerals that your body needs. They also keep your digestive system on track as they contain fibre (essential stuff, which makes sure you poo regularly). Why not make it a mission to try one new kind of fruit every month? Supermarkets or market stalls often have a fantastic selection to choose from.

You could check out how to prepare and cook new vegetables too, and give your taste buds a new sensation! It's fun to experiment with different ways of getting enough of these fab foods, but you don't need to munch a kilo of carrots. Here are some tips to help you get fruit and vegetables into your diet, and there are more on pages 196 to 197. Sorted.

TOP TIPS

- Fresh fruit is full of natural sugars, so eat some when you crave something sweet.
- Frozen vegetables are quick to cook, often cheaper than fresh and full of goodness.
- Open a can of fruit for a quick, easy pudding (but avoid fruit in sweet syrup).
- Keep some crunchy vegetable sticks (carrots and celery are ideal) in the fridge for snack attacks. They'll last for several days in a sealed container and will help fend off the munchies.

We are 100%, total good stuff!

At last, our true worth is recognized.

Meat, fish, eggs, nuts, beans, lentils

Protein (which these foods are jam-packed with) is a healthy body must-have. Your body simply cannot do without it to stay healthy. Some kinds of protein can be pricey (think caviar or fillet steak) but a small chicken breast or a piece of salmon won't break the bank. Luckily, we don't need to eat much protein for our health to benefit.*

The ideas coming up will help you make the most of the protein you eat. A little can go a long way...

* Experts suggest we eat only two or three small portions of protein a day. A portion is two eggs or one small chicken breast. So not that much really.

TOP TIPS

- Avoid frying meat and fish. See if whoever cooks your meals can grill, poach or steam them instead.
- Go for lean meat, or cut the fat off. Most fish is virtually fat-free, or has good, healthy fats. (Fish in breadcrumbs or batter is not as good.)
- A handful of nuts make a great high-protein snack (but avoid salted ones).
- Beans and lentils from cans, cartons or pouches are tasty, quick to cook and just as healthy as dried ones. Add some to stews, curries or soups. Yum!

If you're vegetarian or vegan, you'll find information on how to make sure you get enough protein to keep your body happy and healthy on page 70 and page 74.

Plant-based milks are just as full of calcium as mine!

Milk, cheese and yogurt

These three kinds of food are particularly rich in calcium, which is essential for good health. You'll find calcium in other foods too, such as bread, fish, nuts, broccoli and cabbage, if you're not a fan of dairy. Calcium is vital for building your bones and teeth; making your muscles contract and relax, and making your heart beat. Eat those greens **now!**

Looking good. Must be all that calcium...

Try these ways of getting enough calcium:

TOP TIPS

- If you don't already,
  drink semi-skimmed milk,
  which has half the fat of whole
  milk but the same amount of calcium.
- There are hundreds of different kinds of cheese.
  Why not try some new ones?
- All yogurts are good sources of calcium, but
  go for ones with less sugar, or low-fat Greek
  yogurt that's fabulously creamy.
- Try different ways of eating green veg, such
  as adding some to pasta and soups.

Foods containing fat or sugar

If you find yourself eating lots of cakes, biscuits, crisps and sweets, try seeing them as special treats, rather than regarding them as everyday food. Everyone enjoys a treat, but if you have them all the time, they're not so special any more, are they? Too many of these things can cause weight gain, tooth decay and make you grumpy when the sugar 'hit' you get from them wears off. Sugary, fatty, salty snacks really are **not good** for your health. Sorry.

Are they that bad?

But are fat and sugar really THAT bad? We need to eat some fat to keep warm, build cells in the body and give us essential vitamins. And we know that our body needs to get sugar from food, which it converts into energy. The problem arises when we eat too much of these foods and don't eat enough of the good stuff. Yup, it's as simple as that.

If you often respond to the call of the cake tin, you're not alone, but try these tips to help you cut down on fatty and sugary foods:

I'M OVER HERE

- If you start baking your own, healthier cakes and biscuits you'll know exactly what's in them. There are lots of recipes online.
- Start to check the labels on food to be aware of how much salt, sugar and fat you're eating.
- Don't buy any cakes or biscuits at all. There's zero temptation then.
- Count to 10 before you bite that chocolate bar or doughnut. Will you really feel great if you eat it, or would you actually feel better if you ate something a bit healthier?

Fat

Basically, some kinds of fat are good for you, some are not so good and some are pretty bad:

- The fat in oily fish (such as salmon and tuna), in olive, rapeseed and sunflower oil, and in seeds, nuts and avocados is GOOD for you.

> Experts say that just one portion of oily fish a week is ideal.

- Too much saturated fat, found in foods such as butter, cheese, bacon, sausages, pastry and chocolate is NOT good for you.

- Trans fats are the big baddies (often labelled as 'partially hydrogenated oil'). These lurk in some cooking oils, bought cakes and fast foods. Give them a miss.

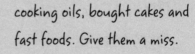

Sometimes, foods like this, that look oh-so healthy, contain lots of fat and sugar:

NUTRITIONAL FACTS

	100g	45g (%RI*)
ENERGY	1972kJ	887kJ (11)
	470kcal	212kcal
FAT	20g	9.0g (13)
of which saturates	4g	1.8g (9)
CARBOHYDRATE	62g	28g
of which sugars	24g	11g (12)
FIBRE	5.4g	

Food labels are complex, but a bowl (45g) of this 'healthy' granola* actually has saturated fat and nearly **three** teaspoons (11g) of sugar in it! Hmm, a nasty surprise.

* Go to Usborne Quicklinks (see page 4) for healthy home-made granola recipes.

The problem with fat

Your body needs fat, but there are lots of reasons why too much of even the good stuff is a bad idea. Basically, if you eat too much fat, you might well:

- Gain weight
- Feel unfit and unconfident
- Feel tired all the time
- Have greasy skin
- Later in your life, you might get heart disease, where fat builds up in the arteries that carry blood around your body and they can't function properly. Bad news.

Why not see if you can reduce the amount of fat you eat by making small changes, such as choosing semi-skimmed milk or low-fat yogurt, for instance? Your body will thank you for it.

Sugar

Some experts think that sugar is the **most harmful** ingredient in our diets today, but, like fat, some kinds of sugar are worse for us than others. The sugar in foods such as cakes, chocolate, biscuits, fizzy drinks and fruit drinks can make us put on weight, rot our teeth and trigger serious health conditions such as obesity and diabetes, especially if we eat too much of it. All of these are growing problems.

A can of cola has so much sugar added to it that dietitians say you shouldn't eat any more sugary food ALL DAY if you drink it.

Uh-oh!

Less is best

There's natural sugar in fruit, vegetables and milk, but these foods are still good for you as they contain vitamins, nutrients and fibre too. Just don't go overboard on fruit and bear in mind that one small smoothie is enough for a day. It's all about **balance**, remember?

There are other options for sweetening what you eat and drink. Some people prefer natural sweeteners such as honey, maple syrup or stevia, but there are also artificial ones such as aspartame (which is often found in fizzy drinks). The best (and cheapest) drink of all is, of course, good old **water**.

Here's one more sugary fact worth knowing: Sadly, because there is now too much sugar in many foods (a lot of it where you wouldn't expect, such as the added sugar in some savoury products) **sugar addiction** is a growing problem. Some people feel that they cannot cope for long without needing to eat something sugary and start to feel awful if they can't. More people are cutting sugar out of their diet as much as they can, fearful of what it's doing to their bodies. Sugar is a big problem for people with the illness diabetes, too.

The best advice is to look at the sugar content in what you're eating, and then try to...

eat as little sugar as you can.

You may find that you soon become used to it and it will be a new, healthy habit. **Hooray!**

Processed foods

There's one more kind of food that wasn't shown among the five food groups you read about at the beginning of this chapter. It's known as 'processed food' and it includes:

Any food that is <u>not</u>
in its natural state,
but has been processed
in some way.

Hmmm. But if you think about it, even food such as cheese has been through several processes to become a block of cheese. (It started off as milk, remember?) The difference between these foods is **how** they are processed and **what's added** to them along the way. It's not always good stuff.

Sometimes, manufacturers add vitamins and minerals to foods such as breakfast cereal. That's usually fine, but a lot of processed food, such as pizzas, sausages, ready meals, chicken nuggets and sweets, have things added to them that are <u>not</u> fine and may even be harmful. Many contain high levels of salt and sugar in particular.

Without wishing to send you on a guilt trip, it's OK to eat some processed foods from time to time, but the best advice really is to **eat as few of them as you can**. If you're in a hurry, a stir-fry might take a bit longer to cook than a pizza or a microwave meal but it can be far healthier. Find more good, quick meals on pages 189 to 192.

Quick quiz

Let's look back at the things you've
just read about. It's important stuff.

Check back through this chapter
to find the answers to these questions.
That will help you remember it all.

1. Can you name three starchy carbohydrates?

2. How many portions of fruit and veg should
   we aim to eat every day?

3. Name three foods packed with protein.

4. List two foods which contain 'good' fat.

How did we do?

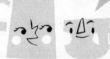

Let's check our answers below...

It takes time to learn good eating habits if you haven't really thought about what you eat before. When you start to learn more about food, you'll make healthier choices. There's lots more info to help you on Usborne Quicklinks (see page 4).

It's time for a NEW you!

1 – Choose from potatoes, bread, pasta, rice or cereals.
2 – At least 5 portions.
3 – Choose from meat, fish, eggs, nuts, beans, lentils.
4 – Choose from oily fish, seeds, nuts, avocados and some cooking oils.

Other diets

Many millions of people make different decisions about what they eat and live by their own food values and principles. Here are some of the main choices they make:

Vegetarianism

Vegetarianism (which means not eating any meat rather than only eating vegetables) is not new. In many parts of the world, most people are vegetarian, but it's becoming more and more popular in countries where most people ate meat in the past. It's all a matter of choice.

I just don't like the taste of meat.

If you are thinking about becoming a vegetarian, it can be a very healthy way to live, but you do need to make sure you eat enough protein. You can get this from:

- **Lentils, chickpeas, soya beans and most other beans** (including baked beans)
- **Eggs** – full of protein, and delicious boiled, scrambled, poached or in other dishes.
- **Yogurt, milk and cheese**
- **Nuts and seeds**
- **Tofu** (made from soya milk)
- **Mycoprotein** (made from fungi, in the mushroom family). It's got no fat in it, but lots of fibre and protein. You can cook it in various different ways.
- **Seitan** (made from wheat gluten). Often called 'wheat meat', seitan is very similar to meat in look and texture when cooked.

Pescatarianism

Great word, isn't it? It means a diet in which you
eat fish (but not meat) and it comes from the Italian
word for fish, *pesce*. Fish, and shellfish such as
mussels, crabs and prawns, are full of protein,
vitamins and minerals. You can buy them fresh,
frozen and canned, and choose from many different
ways of cooking and eating them. Look out for the
words 'sustainably sourced' (which means that the
fish are not caught so intensively that there are
very few left in the water). There are some simple
but tasty fish and seafood recipes at Usborne
Quicklinks (see page 4).

Here are just a few of the most
popular types of fish and
seafood people eat, but
there are plenty more:

MACKEREL CRAB

TUNA HADDOCK

TROUT **COD**

SARDINES **SALMON**

PRAWNS

Veganism

Vegans don't eat anything that is part of,
or comes from an animal, including eggs and cow's
milk. Many vegans don't like to wear anything made
from leather either, such as leather shoes or bags.
They eat what's called a plant-based diet, in which
their food all comes from plants, and instead of
dairy milk, they drink soya, oat, almond, rice or
coconut milk. More people are becoming vegans,
many because of the link between meat production
and climate change: cows produce a gas called
methane which can trap heat in our atmosphere,
adding to global warming.

Veganism can be a healthy way to live but
it's really important to make sure you get
enough protein and vitamins. A vegan diet
sometimes lacks vitamin B12, for instance,
but this is often added to plant-based milks
and cereals, so check if you're not sure.

Vegans get their protein from:

- **Seitan** – made from wheat gluten (so if you can't eat gluten, don't eat seitan).
- **Oats** – porridge is an ideal breakfast for anyone and is quick, filling and healthy.
- **Edamame (soya) beans**
- **Tempeh and tofu** – which are made from soya beans and soya milk.
- **Lentils, chickpeas and most kinds of beans**
- **Spelt, quinoa and hempseed**
- **Nuts and seeds**
- **Green peas** – which are particularly packed with good things. Who knew?

If you use coconut oil, use it in small amounts. It's more than **80% saturated fat** (see page 60).

Organic food

How our food is produced is a hot topic at the moment and many worry that intensive farming is making our food less healthy. Organic food is produced by farmers and growers who avoid man-made chemicals such as pesticides (to kill bugs and pests) or artificial fertilizers (designed to make crops grow better). They don't add anything artificial to their animals' food either: some non-organic farmers routinely add antibiotics, for example, to help prevent their animals becoming ill.

Organic sounds ideal... **but** there is a downside.

There are many places where you can buy organic fruit, vegetables, meat and dairy products and most supermarkets have a wide range. This is all good, but these products can often be more expensive. Also, experts are still unsure whether they benefit our health more than food grown on non-organic farms. Buying organic is really a question of choice and budget, and it's much better to eat non-organic fruit and veg than none at all.

I can't afford organic apples today.

Allergies

If you are allergic to something, such as dust or pollen from plants and flowers, it can make you feel unwell in various different ways. You might develop symptoms such as a rash, a headache, a runny nose or may not be able to stop sneezing. Many people can't eat particular foods without getting some or all of these symptoms.

Health experts are worried that more young people now have conditions such as asthma and eczema (see page 31). There may be many reasons for this, but doctors can do tests to see if you react badly to particular foods, so you can then avoid those ingredients by checking the labels on packaging. If you're eating out, staff should be able to tell you what's in the food, so ask. For a few people, food allergies are so serious that they need to carry medication all the time, so don't think twice: ASK.

Some of the foods that people may be allergic to:

- **Cow's milk and cheese**
- **Eggs**
- **Nuts** that grow on trees (such as brazil nuts, almonds, pecans and walnuts).
- **Peanuts** (which grow under the ground in case you didn't know!)
- **Shellfish and crustaceans** such as oysters, mussels, prawns, lobsters and crabs.
- **Wheat**
- **Soy**
- **Fish**

Luckily there are so many different kinds of food that you won't starve if you're allergic to something here. The most important thing to remember is to aim for a good healthy balance in what you CAN eat and drink, and to avoid too much of anything.

Stress and allergies

We know that stress is bad for our health, but experts now believe that when you're anxious, especially for a long period of time, it can trigger your body to produce the same symptoms as an allergy and can often make these symptoms worse. Whatever makes you react this way, it's worth finding out the cause and trying to see if you can tackle whatever's worrying you. Never feel that you're alone, though. Everyone has times when they feel anxious or worried about things: you'll find all sorts of coping tips in **Chapter 8**.

What about water?

There's one more thing that is absolutely VITAL for your body's good health: **WATER.**

Amazingly, around 60% of your body is water so it's essential you drink to keep replenishing it. If you don't drink enough water, you'll probably be:

- Tired
- Snappy and irritable
- Unable to concentrate
- Having headaches
- Dizzy and spaced-out
- Producing very yellow wee
- Having a dry mouth and smelly breath
- All of these things at once

Doesn't sound like much fun, does it?

How much you need to drink depends on the climate where you live, how old you are and if you are exercising a lot, but most experts agree that, ideally...

We should all drink around 1.2 litres (2 pints) of water <u>every</u> day.

Tap water is usually fine (though it might taste nicer if you use a water filter in some areas) and **free,** so set yourself reminders, carry a refillable bottle and get into the habit of drinking enough.

Healthy food checklist

Now that you've read this part of the book, you're hopefully (no, probably!) wondering how soon you can start making sure you eat as healthily as possible. Yesssssssss!

Turn the page to make that start…

My body really needs this after all that exercise!

Remember, small changes **make a big difference,** so don't feel you have to do everything all at once. Perhaps begin with these five simple tips and see how you get on:

1

For snacks, try a piece of fruit, a handful of nuts, crunchy veg sticks and some low-fat hummus. **Bananas** are a brilliant, filling snack, and full of good stuff.

2

Make sure you **eat some breakfast.** It powers up your body for the day ahead. Try yogurt, fruit and nuts, or porridge with some berries or slices of apple.

3

Don't be afraid to **experiment.**
Try a kind of fruit or vegetable
you've never eaten, or get involved
in cooking a recipe your family
has not tried before.

4

Eat something from
all five food groups
every day. It isn't as difficult as
you think, honestly. You may even
find you do it already.

5

Eat well... but slowly.
You'll taste your food more (and may
eat less) if you don't rush your meals.
It's great to choose healthy food, but
remember to enjoy it too!

Chapter 4

Diets and dieting

Now that you know what's inside your amazing body, how it works, and what makes up a good, balanced diet, you may feel you're sorted. You know all you need to about this area of health and are happy in your own skin. If this is you, that's **fabulous...** but not everyone finds it so easy.

Sadly, some people have a far less positive attitude to food, eating and their bodies. This can lead to depression, and illnesses called eating disorders, which are on the rise, especially among young people. Many people who have these illnesses keep them hidden, but there are ways of spotting someone who's in trouble. One day, this information might help you to help someone else. Check out what to look for on the following pages.

Good diet, bad diet

What do you think about when you hear the word 'diet'? Many people think 'getting thinner', but in fact the word can mean three very different things:

1) Everything you eat to nourish your body is called your diet.

2) A doctor may recommend a specific diet which is, say, low-fat, or cuts out certain foods.

3) Finally, limiting what you eat to try to lose weight is called 'going on a diet'.

...and it's number 3 that can cause problems.

Read this question and then, **honestly,** give your answer:

Have you EVER thought about dieting, been on a diet or wanted to be thinner?   **Yes** or **No**

Well? Did you choose **'Yes'**? The chances are that most of us, at some point in our lives, will want to lose a bit of weight. This is pretty normal, but the problems arise when:

- You start eating less of the vital, good stuff in order to get thin.

- Nobody else thinks that you have any weight to lose, but you do.

- You don't stop dieting when you've lost that weight: you carry on and on...

Maybe I should skip this meal...

I'm happy with my body.

I hate my fat body.

Know someone who might
have a problem with food?

If so, see if you can help
organize some advice and support.

If you're at all worried about your weight, you could
check your BMI* (your 'body mass index') which
tells you whether you are heavier than is healthy,
or not. If you are, it's OK, you can sort it. Here are
four suggestions that might help you begin:

1. Start eating more fruit and vegetables.
    There are so many kinds to try.
2. Cut out sugary snacks and sweet
    fizzy drinks. They really are the bad boys.
3. Gradually reduce the size of your portions
    and eat more slowly. Enjoy your food!
4. Start doing some simple
    exercise, like walking a dog.

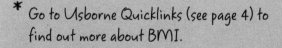

* Go to Usborne Quicklinks (see page 4) to
  find out more about BMI.

Damaging diets

Extreme diets (when you eat so little that your body loses weight very rapidly) or 'fad diets', (where you cut out a whole food group, such as carbohydrates) are growing trends, but worrying ones. They don't work in the long term, and can actually damage your health.

The best advice of all is pretty simple. You should:

Eat a well-balanced diet

Try not to eat too many treats

DRINK LOTS OF WATER

GET ACTIVE

You'll find information and suggestions about all these things in this book. Yay!

If you follow this advice, you'll **feel much better** about yourself in **every way.** It's **life-changing,** and **you're worth it!**

Remember that nobody is, or can ever be, 'perfect': it's much more important to be...

HEALTHY

than THIN.

When things go wrong

Everyone needs enough food to keep their bodies
and brains functioning properly but people who
develop eating disorders can lose sight of that.
For them, food becomes an enemy, and what they
weigh controls how they live their lives, even if what
they are doing is making them ill. These disorders
can really affect people's lives – their health, their
relationships and their work. On the next few pages
are the symptoms of the main disorders people
can have connected with food. Every one of them
can trigger other mental health
problems, such as depression
and anxiety, and all of them
can cause enormous unhappiness.

That's how
I see myself.
Sigh.

Anorexia Nervosa

Probably the best-known eating disorder is anorexia nervosa. Its symptoms are listed here. Although not everyone with anorexia has all these, they are all warning signs.

- They may miss meals, eat very little and avoid any 'fattening' foods.
- They believe (and probably keep saying) that they're overweight when they're not.
- They are very, very thin but may hide this with baggy clothes.
- They may take medication to reduce their appetite or make them poo a lot.
- They may exercise compulsively.
- They will probably have a very lo (body mass index).

Bulimia Nervosa

Bulimia is easy to hide, as people who have this illness may look OK, and are not always very thin. This illness makes them obsessed with controlling how much food is in their bodies and they may develop some or all of the following symptoms:

- They will eat lots of (usually unhealthy) food in a short space of time (or binge).
- They then 'purge' themselves by being sick, or taking medication to make them poo.
- They often exercise obsessively.

They may do all three, one after the other, again and again...

Binge Eating Disorder (BED)

BED can be hard to spot too, as people with it often hide what they are doing. There's only one main symptom, but it's a bad one, as it locks people into an awful cycle of eating, feeling bad, eating to feel better... and so on.

- BED involves sufferers eating huge amounts of food in a short space of time without really enjoying it. Afterwards, they feel uncomfortably full, guilty, sad and ashamed.

Body Dysmorphic Disorder (BDD)

People with BDD become obsessed with what they see as 'flaws' in their body (which others usually can't even see) and have very low self-confidence as a result. They often don't eat well, follow extreme diets, have cosmetic surgery and feel very unhappy (as of course they can never solve problems they haven't really got). The main symptoms of BDD are:

- Talking about their body and its downsides a lot of the time.
- Researching these downsides obsessively.
- Talking about how gorgeous/buff/slim/ perfect everyone else is.
- Not being able to pass a mirror without looking in it and spending a lot of time 'studying' how they look.

What do eating disorders do?

So what effects can these four disorders have on someone's health? Well, bad ones is the short answer. Here are some of them:

- Vomiting and reflux brings up acid from the stomach, which can wear away teeth enamel.
- Hair may fall out and skin become very dry.
- Girls' periods might stop.
- Bingeing can cause weight gain.
- It's really difficult to sleep, so sufferers feel constantly exhausted.
- Constipation (not pooing regularly) leads to smelly breath and a tummy ache.
- It's hard to get warm, so sufferers feel cold all the time.

Now for the good news

So, if you're worried that you, or someone you know, might have some issues about food, weight, body-image and eating, **it's vital to ask for help** as early as possible. Talk to parents or carers, teachers, your GP, or someone you trust. Soon.

If left untreated for a long period of time, eating disorders can lead to **very serious** health problems indeed. Always remember that breaking the cycle of an eating disorder takes time, expert treatment and support, but it <u>can be done</u> and things can and do get better.

I'm so glad those dark times are behind me.

Me too!

Chapter 5

Body maintenance

As well as healthy eating, basic 'body maintenance' goes hand in hand with everything you'll read about in this book, making sure you are as happy and healthy as you can be. If you let things slip, or don't bother for a while, you'll probably start to feel bad about yourself (and you might start to smell as well — sorry, but it's true). Yes, it's time to get up close, and talk about **personal hygiene**.

Hair

How your hair looks can make a big difference to how you feel, and people can spend a lot on their hair. Here are some simple, inexpensive things you can do to avoid ever having a 'bad hair day' again (or at least to cut down your chances of one):

- Make sure you **keep your hair clean**. This doesn't mean washing it every day, but if it gets greasy or smelly quickly, you might need to wash it every two or three days.

- **Use a shampoo that suits your hair type,** and a conditioner too if you like, or if your hair's a bit dry. Nice-smelling products make your hair smell good too. Win, win.

- A **regular trim** is good for your hair, and gets rid of split ends (when the ends of each hair get so dry that they split). Once every two to three months is fine.

- Your hair is a good indicator of how healthy you are. What you **eat**, how much you **sleep** and how **active** you are can all contribute to shiny, healthy hair. Now you know!
- Heated styling tools such as straighteners, and bleaching your hair repeatedly, will **damage** its delicate structure, so avoid them.
- Try out new styles, colours and products if you like (perhaps in the school holidays...) and try to **use good quality products**.
- Remember that nobody else in the WORLD has hair exactly like yours. **Celebrate your unique locks** by keeping them healthy.

TRY THIS...

Circle your fingertips over your scalp to give yourself a **gentle head massage**. It's relaxing, and can stimulate hair growth too!

Skin

Your skin protects your body, keeping it warm when it's cold, and cool when it's hot. It's constantly renewing itself as your body sheds old skin and grows new stuff. Unfortunately, during puberty (when your body is changing into the adult you will become) your skin changes too, and you may get oily areas on your face, as well as some spots. Boo hiss! Here's how to take good care of your skin:

Try to have a good wash of your smelly bits, or a shower or bath, every day. Use soap or shower gel, but not too much. There's lots of stuff out there for sensitive skin.

We all sweat, but you sweat more during puberty. If sweat stays on the skin for too long, it smells, so use deodorant every time you wash your armpits to stay whiff-free.

Spots are perhaps the biggest downside of puberty. They can get you down, but they are part of growing up, so you may have to manage them as best you can.

Turn the page for some questions and answers about spots. If you need more information, there's a huge amount online.

THE SPOT REPORT

Why do I get them?

During puberty (it's that word again, grrrr) your body produces more of an oil called sebum than at any other time during your life. When sebum blocks a pore (a tiny weeny hole in your skin) germs can build up and a red spot may form.

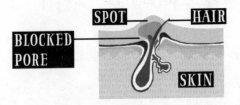

Does everyone get them?

No, but millions and millions of young people do, and always have, so you are not alone. In most cases, they go once your body settles down again after puberty.

How do I deal with them?

This is tricky, and different things suit
different people, but there are some
basic things that it's worth doing:

- **Wash your face morning and night.**
  Use a gentle, antibacterial facewash (no
  facecloths or sponges) and dab your face
  dry with a clean towel, or tissue paper.
- **Eat a balanced diet and drink plenty of
  water.** Water is vital for healthy skin.
- **Try not to pick, squeeze or prod your spots.**
  It's sooooo tempting, but it can make them
  worse and may make them leave a red scar.
- **Try not to focus on them.** Most of your
  friends will be too busy thinking about
  their own spots/wobbly bits/dandruff
  to care that much. Yes, really.

DON'T LET YOUR SPOTS DEFINE YOU.

Sun and your skin

Getting out into the sunshine is good for your body. It helps it make some of the vitamin D you need to keep your bones, teeth and muscles healthy, BUT lying in hot summer sun to get a suntan is not good: it's **dangerous.** The two kinds of ultraviolet light (UVA and UVB) from the sun can burn, wrinkle and weaken your skin, and could even lead to skin cancer. Sunbeds and sunlamps are even worse, so give them a miss.

BUT warm sunshine on your skin feels **great,** and can really cheer you up, so let's look at some basic tips for enjoying sunshine healthily.*

* Go to Usborne Quicklinks (see page 4) to find out more about sun safety.

- Whatever your skin type or colour, **wear sunscreen**, or moisturizer with sunscreen in it, every time you are outside on a bright, or sunny day. Look for those that say SPF (sun protection factor) of at least 30 and have four stars (★★★★) or more. These will give you the best protection against <u>all</u> UV rays.

- If you go swimming, **put more sunscreen on** as soon as you have dried off.

- **Never let your skin be exposed for long enough to start to burn** (because this means it's already damaged).

- **Wear a hat and cover up**, especially during the hottest part of the day, which is usually between 11am and 3pm.

If you have light skin and really want to look tanned, you can avoid skin damage by trying one of these safer methods:

- **Use a self-tanning cream**. There are so many available now. The ones you put on with a sponge mitt are easiest to apply.
- **You could get a spray tan**, perhaps for a special occasion. They don't damage the skin and wear off in a few days. You may find you look more orange than tanned, though!

REMEMBER...

Sun damage not only causes painful sunburn, but can also eventually lead to wrinkles and even skin cancer. It's really not worth taking the risk.

Hands and nails

Think about the **thousands** of things your hands touch, every single day (and, let's face it, not everything they touch is squeaky clean – eeuuurgh!). Here are some handy (haha) tips to help you look after your hands and nails:

Next stop, the sink!

- **Always wash your hands**, with warm water and soap, and dry them properly, after going to the toilet. If the next thing you touch is your mouth, any germs on your hands could make you ill. Yep: it's <u>that</u> important.
- **Keep your nails clean**, and make sure no dirt is trapped under them: not only does this look scuzzy, but it's a paradise for bacteria.
- If you wear nail polish, or have false nails, take them off from time to time with acetone-free nail polish remover and **rub some moisturiser into your nails**.

- **Trim your nails regularly** with a nail clipper or nail scissors. Don't forget your toenails, as they can start to dig into your skin or push against your shoes. Ouch.

- Finally, **eat a healthy, balanced diet**. What you eat really does affect how strong your nails are, their colour and how fast they grow. In fact, foods full of calcium, such as milk and cheese, are like superfoods for nails!

TRY THIS...

For a special treat, have a pedicure (for feet) or manicure (for hands). It's a chance to look after your nails and help make sure that they stay strong, clean and gorgeous.

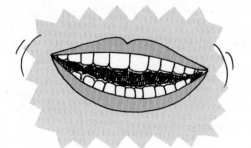

Teeth

Taking good care of your teeth is not difficult, or time-consuming, but it's important. Your 'big' teeth* need to last you your **whole life** (and that's a whole lot of smiling, chewing and chatting). Here are some top tips for good tooth care (but don't try saying that with a mouthful of toothpaste!):

- **Clean your teeth twice a day** (morning and night) with a toothbrush and toothpaste containing fluoride, for two minutes. Time yourself – it's longer than you think.

* The teeth you have when you're a young child are called your 'milk teeth'. They start falling out and being replaced by 'big' teeth at around the age of six.

- Bits of food and bacteria can get stuck between your teeth and cause decay. **Use dental floss or an interdental brush** (a little brush that goes into the gaps between your teeth) every day, to get any bits of food out.

- **Sweets, sugary food and fizzy drinks are particularly BAD**. If you eat or drink them, do so with a meal and then try to brush your teeth about 30 minutes afterwards.

- **Make sure you see your dentist regularly** (ideally every 6 to 12 months, but this can vary) for a check-up. If there is any problem, they can sort it out quickly.

Even if your teeth aren't dazzling white or movie-star perfect, a **happy smile** cheers everyone up.

About braces

If you need braces on your teeth for a while to sort out any problems, it's especially important to keep them clean. Your orthodontist will tell you exactly how to make sure your braces do their job until the wonderful day when they come off. That's the perfect time for a

great big smile.

Chapter 6

Exercise: it really _is_ good for you

How would you answer this question?

> Do you think you're getting enough exercise at the moment?

If you kept a diary for a week of all the active things you do, would it be a bit empty? Do you ever use some of these excuses to avoid doing something energetic or playing a sport?

It's too TRICKY!

I'm too TIRED.

Nope. Too BUSY.

It's too WET!

If this is you, **don't feel bad:** you're not alone and you can change!

I wish we'd started this ages ago!

This part of the book looks at why it matters to be active and how much exercise you really need. (It's probably less than you think, by the way, before you skip this chapter altogether.) Not everyone has a body built for sport, but everyone has a body built to...

MOVE!

If you start building being active into your life, your heart, lungs, muscles, joints, bones, skin and mental health will all thank you for it. **Result.**

Some people have a pretty negative view of exercise, seeing it as something they can't possibly get involved in. Let's start by thinking about what it means to <u>you</u>. Which answer would you pick from these five choices?

1 I love exercising and regularly play some kind of sport.

2 I always feel good when I do some exercise, so I try to do some regularly.

3 I've tried lots of different kinds of exercise, but I don't like any of them.

4 I'm very unfit, so I would much rather chill out and play games or watch films.

5 I never get picked for the team, so what's the point?

Answers

If you chose 3, 4 or 5, don't worry, but it's probably **time for a rethink,** for the sake of your health. As a young person, it's especially important that you get enough exercise and your body is easily capable of doing it. Yes, it might be a bit of an effort at first, but you can start small...

...even **10 minutes** exercise a day is better than nothing.

I've got to start somewhere.

Wow!

If you're still unsure about being active, read these reasons why it can make your life a whole lot better. You might just change your mind.

- **Exercise is good for your body**. It strengthens your heart, bones and muscles and makes it less likely that you'll get ill. Being fit now, when you're young, will help you stay healthy for the rest of your life.

- **Being active makes you feel better**. Your body releases chemicals called endorphins when you exercise, which can help if you're feeling stressed or down.

- **Exercise makes you look better** and feel more confident. Your skin starts to glow, your muscles become more toned and you're less likely to be overweight.

- Going to an exercise class or playing in a team teaches you **valuable life skills** (like patience, co-operation and being, literally, a 'team player').

Whee!

Knowing that your body is fit and healthy, and doing just some of the amazing things it's capable of, is a **really great feeling.** Honestly. If you're unsure, why not find out for yourself?

Wow! I'm so loving this!

Try it and see!

Once you've made up your mind to be more active, there are lots of ways of achieving your goal that don't involve running a marathon. You'll find a list of some things to try on pages 202 to 203 of this book, but the key is to do just that – **try things,** and find what suits you. You're far more likely to give something up if you find it difficult, embarrassing or boring, so keep trying until you find the best fit for you and your life. There will be (at least) one...

It's a good idea to do a variety of different kinds of exercise, if you can. Some activities (like aerobics and team sports) are better for your **heart;** others (like gymnastics and trampolining) build **muscle strength** and some (like yoga and martial arts) are great for **flexibility.** Many forms of exercise do <u>all three</u> of these. Whatever you choose, it's good for your health. **Yay!**

How shall I start?

It's OK if you haven't been very active for a while, but it's important not to overdo things to start with and risk injuring yourself. Experts say that young people should do something active for about an hour a day, but **don't panic:** it's best to build up your fitness gradually, changing some habits and introducing new ones. Everybody works at a different pace and there isn't a set timetable to follow.

Whatever exercise you choose to start, aim to work through each of the three stages (or levels) of exercise intensity shown over the page. This way, you'll gradually increase your stamina (the technical term for the ability to keep on going) and be able to do more and more.

Don't worry! Just try again.

TRY THIS...

Before and after you exercise, it's a good idea to have a **healthy snack** such as those suggested on page 192. You need to put some fuel into the tank before you zoom off!

Stage 1: Light exercise

Here are three very simple everyday changes that will get you on the right track (haha):

- Walk to school if you can (or walk part of the way, at least).
- Ride your bike (if you have one) to the shops or school, instead of getting the bus.
- Put some music on in your room and have a good old dance. Go on — nobody's watching!

Stage 2: Moderate exercise

Next, take things up a notch to 'moderate exercise' (which makes your heart beat a bit faster):

- Walk to school swinging your arms at a comfortable, but fast, walking pace.
- Push those bike pedals a bit faster or go up a gentle hill. You should get a little out of breath.
- Choose one of the many online exercise routines and get that heart rate up!

Stage 3: Vigorous exercise

Right, it's time to try the final level, 'vigorous exercise'. This will get you really out of breath and get your heart beating much faster – but you really do need to **prepare your body each time** and allow it to recover afterwards, if you're going to do it properly. Here's how:

1) Warm up

This is exactly what it sounds like, a way of getting your body warmed up and ready for exercise. It should last at least five minutes, and you should feel warm by the end of it. A good, easy warm-up exercise is to jog on the spot, circling your hands first one way, then the other.

2) Stretch out

Before you start to do vigorous exercise,
such as an aerobics class or a football game,
prepare your muscles to work hard by doing
some dynamic stretches. Dynamic stretches
are gentle repeated movements (such as twisting
from side to side or lifting your knees up high)
which gradually loosen up your muscles.

3) Recover

When you've finished exercising, your body
needs to recover and your heart rate needs to
return to its normal speed. Don't rush this part
of your exercise routine. Slowly stretch out
those muscles and take some good deep breaths.
You'll find lots of stretches to try on Usborne
Quicklinks (see page 4). Walk around for a few
minutes, or until you feel recovered and your
breathing is back to normal. Brilliant!

WHOOSH

Now you know how to tackle doing some vigorous exercise, here are some ideas to try. It's better to go with a friend, and always run or cycle in safe places.

- **Go for a jog** (though perhaps not to school or you'll be sweaty when you arrive). Build up how far, and how fast, you run over a few weeks.

- **Plan a more challenging cycle ride** and push as hard as you can to get round it. You'll feel it in your leg muscles — but hey, be proud that they've worked so hard!

All together

Now you're a whole lot fitter, why not think about
joining a regular exercise class, swimming,
dancing or running club and getting your
endorphin-kick with a group of other
people? (Check the cost is OK
with whoever is paying
first, of course.)

No excuses

So now you know. Exercise* is <u>vital</u> for **good health,** and it actually makes you **feel and look good.**

If you're still a bit worried about not being good enough, or embarrassing yourself, here are **10 ways to get moving** that nobody needs to know about but you. You might need to build up to some of them gradually, but they'll get easier as you get fitter and you'll soon see the benefits to your body:

* Go to Usborne Quicklinks (see page 4) to find out more about exercises to try.

10 WAYS TO MOVE...

1. Do 10 star jumps.

2. Buy a skipping rope, and get skipping.

3. Do five squats (see page 200).

4. If you need to walk somewhere, why not jog or run instead?

5. Make up an energetic dance routine to your favourite tune.

6. Lie flat on the floor and do some stomach crunches (see page 200).

7. Do an online exercise session.

8. Play a computer game that involves movement and effort.

9. Do a 'mini circuit' of five star jumps, five squats and five stomach crunches.

10. Promise yourself that you'll do at least one of these, every day. And stick to it.

OK, let's go!

Chapter 7

Mental health matters

So now you've read all about your body, you're eating super-healthily and are starting to do more exercise: **hooray for you!** This part of the book is about another part of your health that's just as important – **your mental health.**

Put simply, mental health is concerned with your **feelings and moods.***

For young people, these can both be pretty stormy.

Today is not a good day.

* Go to Usborne Quicklinks (see page 4) for more about feelings and moods.

Did you know that there's a small but vital difference between 'feelings' and 'moods'?

Feelings, or **emotions,** tend to be a <u>response</u> to something, be it good or bad, and can come and go quickly.

Moods can come out of nowhere, for <u>no reason</u>, hang around and ruin a perfectly good day.

Also in the mental health mix are chemicals that the body produces, called hormones. These make young people very prone to what are called **mood swings** (when moods change very rapidly and dramatically). Sound familiar?

Your mental health is a key part of your overall wellbeing, but a busy life, social media, school, exams and even well-meaning parents can all combine to make you feel overwhelmed at times. Yes, there's a lot more pressure on young people now than in the past, but most also find it easier to **talk about these things,** which is very positive. Good mental health is now recognized as vitally important, so let's find out a bit more about it, and what to do when it's <u>not</u> so good...

I'm sorry you're having a bad day.

This chapter looks at the most common mental health problems that affect young people, so that you know how to recognize any signs of them in yourself, or in others. In **Chapter 8**, you'll find suggestions for staying well mentally and being fully in tune with your emotions (the helpful and the not-so-helpful ones). This area (often called your emotional wellbeing) is a **massive** subject. You'll find lots more information on Usborne Quicklinks (see page 4), but here are the basics, to start with.

Feelings, or emotions, are probably the most complicated part of being human, and they have a **huge** impact on our lives. Let's start by looking at where they come from in the first place...

...your brain.

Brain power

It's usually fairly easy to tell if
your body isn't healthy: you feel
ill and might have nasty symptoms
such as a high temperature, pain or a rash.
You know that your body needs to heal and
repair itself, with or without the help of health
professionals. It can be harder to judge your mental
health, however, as the symptoms can take longer
to develop, are trickier to spot and are controlled
by something you can't see – your brain.

Your brain is a truly amazing thing, even though
it's only about the same size as a cauliflower.
It's a **powerhouse of activity, 24/7,**
and is busy even when you're asleep.

Here are just a few of the things your brain
does without you knowing a thing about it:

- It helps you understand what you see,
  smell, hear, taste and touch.
- It controls how you move parts of your
  body, such as your arms and legs.
- It enables you to feel emotions,
  such as love, happiness and sadness.
- It remembers stuff (which is why older people
  may forget things: their brains are older too).
- It regulates your heart rate, blood flow
  and your breathing.
- It thinks thoughts, asks questions and
  wonders about stuff – ALL the time.

Your brain is seriously
AWESOME, people.

Feelings

We all have **lots** of feelings, often several in a short period of time. Unconvinced? Think back over the past few days, and then put either a real or a mental tick in the circle next to the feelings you've felt during that time:

○ HAPPY   ○ EXCITED

○ SAD   ○ SHY

○ ANGRY   ○ SCARED

○ SURPRISED   ○ JEALOUS

○ WORRIED   ○ STRESSED

○ EMBARRASSED   ○ ANNOYED

I was **happy** I passed the test, but **sad** you failed.

Thanks. I was **annoyed** at first, but not any more.

136

How did you do?

If you ticked just one, that's OK (if unusual) but don't worry if you ticked every single one. It's healthy to have all kinds of feelings: they make us humans human. Many stories are based around the idea that characters who seem to have no feelings actually have lots. **Feelings are good,** and we need them to live as fully and happily as we can, but problems begin when you're always feeling sad, down, or hopeless. If this goes on for a long time, it can be a sign that your mental health is perhaps not as good as it could be.

How does it feel?

Thank goodness there's a growing awareness of how **important** our mental health is. It's not always been easy for people to talk about their feelings, worries and weaknesses: they were often told to 'cheer up', 'snap out of it', or 'get on with life like the rest of us'. Could you do this if you were ill? Of course not: you'd need help.

It can be tricky to describe how you feel if you're very low. Some people even self-harm because they just can't find another way to express pain.

Self-harm

People who self-harm hurt themselves deliberately (usually by cutting) because they feel it brings relief from sadness... but it usually makes it worse. Talk to your GP if you have <u>ANY</u> worries about self-harm.

Most of us know someone who is struggling, or has struggled, with their mental health. They need and deserve just as much sympathy, understanding and support as someone with a physical illness, such as flu. There can be a wait for professional help, but if you think it's needed, ASK for it.

There are many kinds of mental health difficulties – some more severe than others. They can all make life **very miserable** indeed. There are three that often affect young people and they are:

DEPRESSION

ANXIETY

STRESS

Depression

People who have suffered from depression often describe it as: 'everything seems black' or 'like living inside a glass box'. They have no energy, no enthusiasm, no appetite and no interest in doing things they used to enjoy. They may not care about their appearance and often don't sleep well. They also might believe that they will never be happy again.

A lot of people are naturally a bit pessimistic, and others might feel a bit fed up a lot of the time, but depression is much more serious: it's a very real illness. So what triggers it? Well, it can be nothing specific, but more usually it's a response to all kinds of things and it slowly grows until it's like a huge tidal wave of sadness. Not good news.

Possible causes, or triggers, of depression:

- Big pressures or worries, such as serious illness.
- Comparing yourself with others, and feeling you're never good enough.
- A sad life event, such as a relationship break-up, trouble at home, parents separating or the death of someone close to you.
- Depression can run in families, unfortunately.
- Loneliness. Being lonely is a major cause of depression in people of all ages.
- A horrible combo of these things (which alcohol or drugs make lots worse).

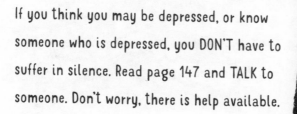

If you think you may be depressed, or know someone who is depressed, you DON'T have to suffer in silence. Read page 147 and TALK to someone. Don't worry, there is help available.

Anxiety

Everyone feels worried sometimes: it's natural and can actually protect you from making bad decisions, or motivate you to work harder for a test. But when anxiety is not helpful, or takes over your life, it's more serious. People suffering from anxiety feel worried, nervous, unsure, insecure, panicky or fearful – or all these things at once – all, or a lot of the time. Different people experience different levels and different kinds of anxiety but for some it gets so severe that they can't even go outside.

Here are the main kinds of anxiety disorder (often linked in a double or triple whammy):

- **General Anxiety Disorder** (or GAD): you worry about things all the time.
- **Obsessive Compulsive Disorder** (or OCD): you feel something bad will happen if things aren't done in a certain way, so you have to keep doing them, again and again...
- **Phobias**: you have an overwhelming fear of something, such as spiders, small spaces or the dark.
- **Panic attacks**: you have a sudden overwhelming feeling of fear, often involving shaking, sweating and gasping for breath.
- **Social anxiety**: you have an intense fear of social situations, which may include worrying about people judging or not liking you.

Stress

You will have read a bit about stress, and what causes it, on page 19 of this book. Some stress is normal, natural, and even good (as it gets us motivated to do things) but too much of it causes a lot of real unhappiness.

The symptoms can be very similar to those of anxiety and are the result of your brain trying to deal with too many pressures at once and going into 'overdrive'. Stress can make your heart race, make it difficult to breathe, stop you sleeping and leave you feeling constantly on edge. Miserable, eh?

Eek! My new school starts tomorrow...

Stress is usually triggered by a build-up of problems, such as:

- A period of worry, or pressure, such as exam time.
- Having too many things to deal with at the same time.
- Always feeling you have to be more attractive/fit/popular than others.
- Never wanting to miss out on anything and so getting exhausted.

Now you know what mental health problems can look like and how serious they can be. In the next chapter, we'll look at what to do if you feel that you, or someone you know, might need help with their mental health. Yup, it's time to get positive!

Chapter 8

Help is out there...

Everyday stresses don't always lead to the problems described in the previous chapter, but if you, or someone you know, has any or all of the symptoms you read about there, it might be time to get some help (especially if things have not been good for a while). Everyone feels a bit wobbly from time to time, or finds things difficult to cope with, and that's **absolutely normal,** but there are ways of helping ensure that these little problems don't grow into big ones.

We are surrounded by different pressures and it can be all too easy to feel overwhelmed or inadequate, but if you start to feel like this, these six steps could stop things getting out of hand. They seem very simple but **they really can work,** so why not give them a go?

1 The first thing to do is to **TALK ABOUT IT**. If you don't tell anyone how you're feeling, nobody will know until it's become a really BIG problem. Getting a doctor's appointment may be tricky, but tell your parent, carer, a trusted friend, a teacher or a school counsellor as soon as you can. Just talking may make you feel better.

I will always help if I can.

I feel better now I've told you.

2 Make sure you're eating and drinking healthily (see **Chapter 3** of this book for more info). The food you put into your body affects your mood, and not enough food, or too much sugary, salty food can leave you with no energy, and unable to concentrate.

3 **Get enough sleep.**
Experts reckon young people
need **8 to 10 hours** good
sleep a night. Yes, really. Find out
more about the importance of sleep to
your physical and mental health in **Chapter 9.**

4 **Do something active every day,** preferably
outside in the fresh air. There's been lots of research
about how exercise helps fend off depression, and
a walk in the park or to the shops is FREE. Even
dancing around your room
can make you feel better.

This feels **good**!

5 Do things you like doing. If you love getting lost in a book, that's great (as long as you talk to people as well!). Doing stuff you enjoy is excellent for lifting your mood and helping you face things you don't enjoy much, but have to do.

6 Make sure you spend time with your friends and your family. Being with other people can stop you brooding about worries and problems and remind you that, however you're feeling, people really care about you.

As well as these six key tactics, there are other ways of taking care of your mental health that are pretty easy to make happen. They may seem obvious but they can make a **huge** difference to how you feel.

RELAX

Most young people lead very busy lives with lots of demands on them. If you try working on different ways of relaxing, switching off your worries for a while, your brain will appreciate the down time and it will **recharge your batteries.** Here are some tips to try:

- **Arrange to spend a bit of time with mates after school** rather than getting straight into all that homework.

- **Download an exercise app, go to an exercise class or stream one.** Build it into your weekly routine and don't find excuses to skip it.

- **Put a limit on your screen time.** Catch up with friends or play a game for half an hour, then switch the screen off and cook, read, do homework, sing, draw or walk the dog. It's good to shut down all the chattering voices for a while.

- **Press the pause button on life for 10 minutes.** Sit somewhere quiet, breathe deeply, focus on what you can see, hear and smell and just let yourself BE.*

- **Set up a good, restful routine before you go to sleep at night.** That way, your mind and body begin to learn when it's time to switch off and relax.

* This is a technique from 'mindfulness'. Find out more on pages 204 to 205, and on Usborne Quicklinks (see page 4).

RESET

It's easy to get into the habit of feeling you're not 'good enough' and that everyone else is cleverer/fitter/having more fun than you. It's never true, but it can trigger real unhappiness and leave you feeling anxious all the time. Changing or 'resetting' these negative habits takes time but it can be done. It can really help to try to **see** the reality, rather than what you **think** is the reality.

Are you always criticizing yourself? Instead of negative things, **think positive things** (and say them out loud, see page 42) such as 'I'm doing great' or 'I'm very good at football'. Be as realistic and kind to yourself as you would be to a friend.

Do you feel that people are always looking at or thinking about you? **Think again.** Most of them are too busy worrying about themselves. Do you spend all your time thinking about other people? Of course you don't, neither do they.

Do you compare yourself with other people and get depressed when you see those perfect pics they post? **Stop and think** about what you post. Does it really tell the full truth about you, or is it all a bit of an act sometimes? Yep? Well, there you go.

RESILIENCE

Put simply, 'resilience' means 'the ability to recover from setbacks or problems' and we all need some of it to get through life. Sometimes being resilient isn't easy but, like any skill, it does get stronger with practice. Here are some ways of developing more resilience to cope with life's ups and downs:

- **Try to be as hopeful and positive as you can, and see the good in things and in people.** A positive, upbeat attitude opens up more opportunities than a negative, defeatist one.

- **When the going gets tough, your best friends and your family are the people you are going to need to talk to.** They may all drive you crazy, but they care about you more than anyone else does. Honestly.

- **If life seems overwhelming, make a list of your worries and ways to tackle them.** Dealing with them one at a time is easier than all at once, and will make you feel back in control much faster.

MY STEPS TO CHANGE
THINGS FOR THE BETTER...
1) ~~Do homework on time~~ ☑
2) ~~Practise the piano~~ ☑
3) Read in bed every night ☐
4) Talk to my mates more ☐

- **Look back at how you've responded to stressful things in the past.** Did whatever you did work, or is there a better way you could try next time? Learn from your mistakes.

Quick quiz

Hopefully you now feel better equipped to tackle the tough times everyone faces now and again. To check, let's see how you would answer these **four important questions...**

1. **Which of these options do you think shows the healthiest attitude to life?**
    a) I'm sorted. Nothing will ever go wrong for me.
    b) Life and people disappoint me all the time.
    c) Sure, life can be tricky, but I always try to stay as positive as I can.

2. **If you're feeling really anxious, what's the best thing to do?**
    a) Organize a really hard challenge to take your mind off it.
    b) Eat loads of chocolate to cheer yourself up.
    c) Talk to someone you trust about how you feel.

3. What should young people do for 8 to 10 hours a night?

a) Go on social media, in case you miss out.

b) Study, revise, do schoolwork and slog.

c) Sleep. Zzzzzzzzzzzzzzzzzzz...

4. Which of these is the best plan, if you've got lots of schoolwork to do?

a) Keep on going until you get absolutely everything done. All night if necessary.

b) Forget it and do something else instead.

c) Finish as many tasks as you can, taking regular breaks. Accept that's all you can do.

If you chose mostly c) answers, **well done.** You're really getting your mental health into good shape. (If you didn't, read the last two chapters again NOW!)

Chapter 9

The importance of sleep

Sleep is just as important as food is for good health. If you don't get enough sleep, your body won't be functioning as well as it should, you'll probably feel very low and you could even get ill. **Sleep is essential,** but do you sometimes think of it as something boring and a bit of a waste of time? If you do, think again. When you're asleep, your body is still growing and developing, recovering from the day, laying down memories and 'rebooting', ready for tomorrow. Pretty important then, isn't it?

How much sleep?

Every night, your body goes through different stages, or levels, of sleep. You start in a light sleep, then go into a deeper sleep and finally move into lighter sleep again. All good, except when you're woken up at the wrong place in this cycle... something that happens to young people **all the time.** Read on to find out why.

Experts believe that young people need between 8 and 10 hours sleep <u>every night</u>. As many schools start at 8.30am, this means they need to go to sleep at around 10/10.30pm, but **their brains are not ready** to sleep then. During puberty, the body follows a slightly different timetable. At 10.30pm, most young people are very wide awake. Uh-oh.

Falling asleep may be tricky, but waking up in the morning can be **even worse,** as the dreaded alarm goes off when teenagers are still in the 'deep sleep' part of their cycle. Here's why:

Melatonin

In the evening, our bodies produce a hormone called melatonin, which helps us prepare for sleep. Young people's bodies don't release melatonin until later in the evening, which is why they aren't ready to sleep until then.

The Get Some Zzzzz's Quiz

It's time to do the quick quiz on the next page to find out if you are getting enough sleep or not...

Quick quiz

1. Do you find it hard to fall asleep at night?

   Yes   No   Sometimes

2. Do you wake up exhausted each morning?

   Yes   No   Sometimes

3. Do you want to fall asleep in lessons?

   Yes   No   Sometimes

4. Are you always tired?

   Yes   No

 Well, if you answered '**Yes**' to two or more of these questions, you're probably **very tired,** all the time. Horrible.

If you're worried, try keeping a 'sleep diary' for a week, to see how long you <u>actually</u> sleep each night. (Many people underestimate this, so try to be honest.)

Always tired?

Being tired is grim, and if it goes on too long, it's **bad for your health.** Here's why:

- While you sleep, your body releases hormones that help you develop. If you don't sleep enough, your development may suffer.
- You may get bad skin (yep, the dreaded spots) and dark circles under your eyes.
- It's easy to feel low, lack confidence, and make mistakes if you're exhausted.
- You'll be moody and less able to concentrate if you're tired. This is bad for a) schoolwork b) family harmony and c) friendships.

Do you know what time it is?

I just couldn't wake up.

Basically, being tired is **rubbish,** so be kind to yourself if this is how you feel a lot of the time.

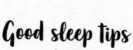

Good sleep tips

There is **hope,** however. There are lots of things you can do to help get enough good, quality sleep.*
Here are seven tips to begin with:

1) NO energy drinks and NO tea or coffee after lunch.

2) Don't eat lots, too late. Give your body a chance to digest your meal before you sleep.

3) Get some exercise and fresh air every day.

4) Stick to a bedtime routine – get into PJs, clean your teeth and go to bed at roughly the same time. This helps your body wind down.

5) Avoid napping. Power through to bedtime.

6) Try a warm bath, a milky drink, or sprinkle a few drops of lavender oil on your pillow. Mmmm.

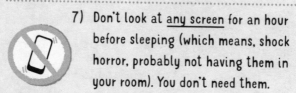

7) Don't look at <u>any screen</u> for an hour before sleeping (which means, shock horror, probably not having them in your room). You don't need them.

---

* Go to Usborne Quicklinks (see page 4) for more tips to get good, quality sleep.

Snacks to help you sleep

It's true – some foods really can help your body wind down in the evening. Try some of these snacks for some serious zzzzs:

➡ A bowl of cereal and milk

➡ Yogurt sprinkled with granola

➡ Toast with a mashed banana on top

➡ A peanut butter sandwich

Room for sleep

Where you sleep is important too. Making sure your bedroom is a comfortable, relaxing place, and preparing yourself for sleep is called 'sleep hygiene'. Cool, eh? Try the tips on the next page to prepare your bedroom for a good night's rest...

Make sure your room is nice and dark. Thick curtains or blackout blinds are ideal.

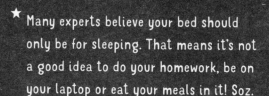

Where you sleep shouldn't be either too hot or too cold. A comfortably cool room is best for sleeping, so keep your window open a crack if you can.

Many experts believe your bed should only be for sleeping. That means it's not a good idea to do your homework, be on your laptop or eat your meals in it! Soz.

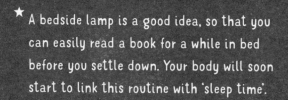

Research shows that a warm, snuggly duvet and a soft, comfortable pillow can help you get better sleep.

A bedside lamp is a good idea, so that you can easily read a book for a while in bed before you settle down. Your body will soon start to link this routine with 'sleep time'.

It's harder to relax in a messy, whiffy room, so if you have dirty clothes on the floor, pick them up before you go to bed.

Sleep and mood

The amount of good, restful sleep you get has an effect on your mood as well as your body. **Life is always busy,** and if you're tired, it's harder to cope, but worrying about things can stop you sleeping and make you even more tired! **Argh!**

Here are some tips to help you stop unhelpful thoughts whizzing around your head:

- **Get everything organized for the next day, before you settle down to sleep.** Pack your school bag, get your clothes ready and set your alarm.

- **If you have things on your mind at bedtime, write them in a notebook before you get into bed.** Worrying about them all night really won't help, honestly.

- **Keep the notebook near your bed**, so that if any worries surface during the night, or you think of solutions (as sometimes happens) you can jot them down and then forget about them until the morning.

- **Don't panic if you can't sleep**. Your body will still be resting and recharging. Breathe deeply and try to let your body relax and sink down into that soft, warm bed.

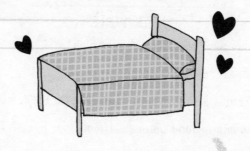

It takes time for the suggestions in this chapter to kick in, but **don't give up**. If you follow them, your body will respond and you'll start to sleep better, feel better, and be ready for what each day brings.

Chapter 10

Other people

Now you know that 'being healthy' is a whole lot more than 'not being ill'. It's more than your diet, exercise levels and general wellbeing, too. There's one more important thing in the mix: other people.

> Your health involves
> the people around you
> as well.

No, it's not all up to you. This chapter looks at how the people around you can affect your health and happiness in good (and not so good) ways.

Home sweet home

Your parents or carers have looked after you
all your life, but now you're growing into
an adult, things are different and you may
not always accept or agree with the way
they do things. For example, they might:

- Impose rules on you that you don't
  want to follow (like 'be home by 10pm').
- Expect you to do things you don't want
  to do (like go to Aunt Flo's party).
- Stop you doing things you <u>do</u> want to do
  (like go to a festival with your mates).
- Cook meals you don't want to eat
  (because, say, you want to be vegetarian).

These things can cause such friction that it
becomes hard for you to talk to your parents or
carers about your worries. This makes them feel
rejected and hurt, so **everyone's miserable.**

Many, many families go through a tricky time during these years: they argue, slam a lot of doors and say things to each other that they don't mean. It usually passes as you settle down after the storms of puberty and everyone realizes that you're now an adult, but it can be stressful at home until then.

I've got a problem...

Try as hard as you can to keep the lines of communication open. It's always best to tell your parents/carers if you are worried about something: they really do want you to be safe and happy you know! If you quarrel, accept apologies graciously and don't be too proud to say sorry yourself if you've gone too far. It <u>will</u> all calm down in the end. Always remember that **families are for life** (however weird you might think yours is).

I'm always here for you.

Friends

We all need good friends. In fact, you may feel that they are a lot easier to talk to than your family during this time in your life and that's 100% OK. A friend can have a HUGE impact on your life, so let's start by thinking about what you look for in a **good** friend. Do you choose your friends well?

We were meant to be mates.

Well, we do seem to have a lot in common...

Quick quiz

Which of these things do you look for in a friend? Answer as **honestly** as you can.

- They are kind
- They share your interests
- They support you when you're down
- They laugh at your jokes
- They understand when you don't feel like chatting
- They share your taste in some things, such as snacks, clothes and box sets

Hopefully you chose EVERY SINGLE ONE of these options, as <u>all</u> these qualities are important in a friend. You could probably add more, too.

But what about you? How do **YOU** measure up? Time to answer some questions about yourself...

Quick quiz

Answer these
questions about
what kind of
friend **you** are:

1. You overhear someone being nasty about
    your friend. Do you...

a) Ignore it and walk away.

b) Tell that person to stop being so unkind.

c) Listen in and tell your friend the goss later.

2. Two of your friends have had a fight.
    Do you...

a) Tell them both to stop being stupid.

b) Talk to each one of them and try to help
    them sort out the problem.

c) Leave them to it: it's their business.

3. **A friend is having a tricky time. Do you...**

a) Tell them to stop brooding.

b) Offer to listen if they want to talk.

c) Talk about your problems to take their mind off their own.

4. **A friend has not done as well in a test as you have. Do you...**

a) Tell them it's cool and doesn't matter.

b) Offer to go through the stuff in the test with them.

c) Say that they probably didn't work hard enough.

If you chose mainly b) answers, **yay!** You're a **great friend,** willing to go the extra mile for your mates. If you didn't, think how you'd feel if your friends behaved like a) or c).

'They made me do it!'

One of the greatest worries young people
have is that they're **different**, or that they
don't fit in with others around them (often called
their 'peers'). At times, it can be tempting to
do things you don't want to because <u>not</u> doing
so means you'll get teased, or left out. This is
called **peer pressure** and it can be a very
powerful pressure indeed. It may be about:

Drinking alcohol

Taking drugs

Having sex when you don't feel ready

Bullying someone (verbally or physically)

Not a nice list, is it? You'll find more information
about all these issues on Usborne Quicklinks
(see page 4) but let's look at the basics here...

Alcohol

The age at which young people are allowed to buy alcohol varies. In the UK, for example, it's **18 years old** (but many shops have a 'think 25' policy, only selling to those who can prove they're 18 or older). These laws are made for good reasons. Alcohol is a **harmful, highly addictive substance** that really changes the way you think and feel. It can make you lose control, make bad choices and leads to a lot of embarrassment.

There's plenty of research into the damage alcohol does to young people's developing brains, and it's best not even to try drinking it until you are at least 15 years old. If it isn't either a sensible or a healthy choice, why not just avoid drinking it?

Drugs

You may be tempted to try drugs or feel pressurized to do so. The truth is that if a medicine is prescribed by a doctor, or bought from a pharmacy and properly used, it's fine, but drugs from anywhere else are **dangerous**, probably **illegal** and could **really harm you.**

Some drugs can affect you very badly and make you deeply unhappy. Some are so addictive that one bad decision can affect <u>years</u> of your life. If someone wants you to experiment with drugs, say **'no'**, as the vast majority of young people do. Your life's far too important to risk it, surely?

Sex

Sex is not just a physical, bodily act, like doing a handstand or throwing a ball. It's personal, and should never be something anyone is pressurized into. Nobody has the right to touch, or make any sexual demand of you if you don't want it. This includes sexting (urging others to send photos of parts of their bodies). These stay in the cloud FOREVER...

Sex is **important** and laws exist to protect young people from having it before they are ready. Some diseases are passed on through sex, and it can lead to pregnancy, after all. Serious stuff. Whatever your peers are doing (or say they're doing) if you feel you don't want to have sex, it's absolutely <u>your decision</u>.

I know I'm just not ready.

Bullying

Bullying (where someone is picked on by others) is horrible and it's on the rise. It can be done face-to-face (such as teasing, leaving people out, wrecking their stuff or insulting them) or on the internet, when it's called cyber-bullying. If anyone tries to get you to become a bully, be the better person and **refuse.** If you, or someone you know, is being bullied, tell someone about it.

<u>NOBODY</u> has the right to bully **ANYONE.** Full stop.

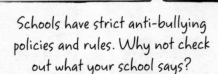

Schools have strict anti-bullying policies and rules. Why not check out what your school says?

Survival tactics

So now you know some of the main 'danger areas' where you could be pressurized by your peers into doing something risky, or that you don't want to, but **don't panic.** There are tactics for coping with peer pressure coming up over the page. It's hard to say **'no'** and fight back. You might need to be pretty brave, but real friends will accept your choices. You may even make them think twice about their choices, and what they see as 'fun'. Doing the right thing is not always easy, but it is always best.

Now this is what I call FUN!

The Good Times Rollercoaster

PEER PRESSURE TACTICS...

1 Just say 'no', and walk away.

NO!

2 Remind your friends of the consequences.
Is getting arrested really going to be a laugh?

3 Tell your friends that **YOU** are in charge
of what you do, not them.

4 If something bad, such as a crime, is planned,
tell an adult, who might be able to prevent it.

5 Suggest an alternative that's not risky,
nasty or illegal. A much better idea.

Above all, remember that you are entitled to <u>your
own opinion</u> and to make <u>your own decisions</u>. The
only person who decides what you do about all the
issues in this part of the book should be **YOU**.
True friends will respect you for being strong.

Bad news overload

There's one more way in which other people can affect your mood, your happiness and generally get you down: by telling you endless worrying news stories. It can be easy to feel **bombarded** with terrible problems, massive world issues and sad stories. Especially when they are beamed into our living rooms and onto our phones and computers every single day. Constant media chatter about climate change, war, disease and political squabbles can **get inside your head** and even affect your mental health. This doesn't help anyone, least of all you. So what can you do about it?

If you can, do something pro-active about the issues that matter to you. You could:

➡ Join a group pressing for change

➡ **Volunteer to help with a charity**   ➡ SIGN A PETITION

This will make you feel as if you are at least doing **something** because feeling completely powerless is distressing. You could also block sites or remove apps that upset you. Overall, try not to get drawn into arguments and problems that you simply cannot solve, however much you care about them.

As this book keeps on telling you, staying healthy is all about getting the balance right.

HEALTH FOR LIFE

The tips and ideas in this part of the book add to what you've already read and aim to help you build what you've learned about good health into your everyday life.

None of these ideas is complicated, expensive, time-consuming or wacky. Even if you only try some of them, it could make a **BIG** difference to how **healthy you are** and how **happy you feel.**

The tips and ideas are divided into sections:

More about **FOOD**

So, nutrition experts recommend that we eat...

at least <u>5</u> portions of fruit and veg EVERY day.

Don't panic! This may sound like a lot, but a 'portion' is not that big, and would probably fit in the palm of your hand. To give you an idea, 2 kiwi fruits, 1 pear, 3 heaped tablespoons of peas or half a red pepper are each one portion.

How many portions have you had today?

Now let's see how you could easily reach that '5-a-day' target:

Add berries to your breakfast cereal or porridge. (Frozen ones are fine and often cheaper). Tasty, filling AND healthy! Perfect.

Top your breakfast toast with a sliced banana instead of a sugary spread.

Add a big handful of salad to your sandwich. Any type will do. Spinach is particularly good.

Aim (gradually if necessary) to fill at least a third of your plate with veg at each meal. Yes, they are THAT good for you and THAT important.

For snacks, try carrot sticks, a handful of grapes, nuts or some cherry tomatoes.

Grate carrot or courgette into soups or casseroles, or chuck in a handful of chopped kale.

Try Greek yogurt and fruit for pudding.

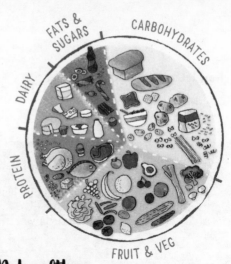

Quick AND healthy

Remember this guide from page 48, showing the proportion of the five food groups you should aim to eat? Well, here are some ideas to get you started on doing just that. They all are quick, easy and **healthy.** It's fine to eat less healthy stuff as a treat, though: we all need a treat from time to time, and life without them would be pretty dull. As ever, it's all about getting the balance right.

Honestly, once you really start **thinking** about what you eat and putting more good stuff into your body, you'll probably never look back!

SPICY SWEET POTATO WEDGES

Potatoes aren't a 5-a-day veg, but sweet potatoes are. Do you gobble unhealthy snacks and find they don't satisfy you? Well, a bowlful of these will – and they'll be worth waiting for.

- Peel the sweet potatoes, and cut them up into wedges.

- Drizzle with a little olive or vegetable oil, sprinkle with a little salt, pepper, paprika and chilli (if you like it).

- Bake in a hot oven (180°C/350°F) for about 25 minutes, until they are soft inside and crispy on the outside.

- Eat with light mayonnaise or 'reduced salt and sugar' ketchup for dipping.

QUICK MINI-PIZZAS

This healthy snack takes minutes to make
and has **carbohydrate, protein** AND **vegetables**
– the three key food groups.

- Toast a slice of bread.

- Spread with tomato puree or passata
  (a ready-made sauce of tomatoes
  sieved to remove the pips and skin),
  add olives, grated cheese, chopped
  cherry tomatoes or sliced tofu. Yum!

- Pop under the grill until the cheese
  is hot and bubbling, and enjoy.

Adapt this recipe with a hunk of crusty
French bread, if you prefer.

I could try this with a pitta bread.

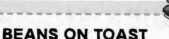

BEANS ON TOAST

Did you know that baked beans can be one of your 5-a-day portions? Ones with less salt and sugar are best of all. Easy peasy (or 'beansy').

- Heat up at least 3 tablespoons of beans in the microwave or in a saucepan.

- Toast some bread (wholemeal is best).

- Pour the beans onto the toast.

- Sprinkle a little grated cheese on top if you like.

- Eat with a handful of crunchy salad for even more good stuff.

A delicious, filling and healthy lunch or snack in under 5 minutes – result!

≡ QUICK SNACKS

Snacking is sooo tempting. If you're peckish, instead of crisps or biscuits, try these ideas:

- **MICROWAVE POPCORN**

  The plain variety is the healthiest.

- **A BOWL OF WHOLEGRAIN, LOW-FAT CEREAL**

  Who said it's only great at breakfast time?

- **A BANANA**

  Full of good stuff, filling and high in energy.

- **CELERY STICK SPREAD WITH PEANUT BUTTER**

- **A FRUIT SMOOTHIE**

  Add any fruit you like, fresh, canned or frozen (but not <u>too</u> many smoothies, remember?).

What if I'm vegan?

Well, here are some tips for **you!** A vegan diet can be healthy, but it's very important to make sure that you include **protein** with <u>at least two</u> of your daily meals.

If you ask whoever buys the food in your house to get a few vegan basics for you, it's easier than you think to adapt family recipes: you just need to plan a little more. If you substitute vegan cheese, you can make **all** the snacks in this chapter, for example. As for main meals, try making meatless bolognese or chilli sauce, burgers and spicy patties with vegan mince. Just cook your portion in a pan alongside the version for 'non-vegans' in your family. Remember to add lots of seasoning, vegetables and/or pulses (onions, peppers, garlic, tomatoes, chickpeas, kidney beans). **Delicious** and **very healthy**!

A glass of water with lunch will help me concentrate afterwards. Yay!

Make your own lunch

Packed lunches can be the least healthy meal of the day, if you're not careful, as they are often crammed with processed food. Remember that brown or seeded bread has more goodness in it, or why not try wholewheat wraps, or pitta bread? If you make your own packed lunch the evening before school, you can make sure that it's a) healthy and b) a bit different each day.

Vegetarians and vegans will need to adapt the following options (with vegan cheese, for instance) but why not give some of these combos a try?

- A grated cheese, lettuce and sliced tomato sandwich
- Sliced cold chicken/ham or tofu and salad wholewheat wrap
- Hummus or tuna salad in a wholemeal pitta
- Cooked cold pasta with chopped peppers, carrots and sweetcorn, stirred in with a spoonful of light mayonnaise. Add cubes of ham, cheese or tofu too, if you like.
- Banana and nut butter wholemeal sandwiches
- Grated carrot and sliced apple salad bowl

- Crumbled feta cheese and salad in a flatbread

For extras, instead of a sweet biscuit or packet of crisps, you could have a handful of nuts, a low-fat yogurt, a piece of fruit, or a hard-boiled egg – or why not **try ALL** of them?

Tried and tested

If you aim to eat some kind of fruit or veg with every meal, you'll soon nail your 5-a-day target. Can you add up how many of the things on this list you've already tried and know you like? If there are any you didn't like, why not try them again, but in a different way? Your friends might have some recipe ideas you can try out together.

THE **FRUIT & VEG** CHECKLIST

FRUIT

- apples
- bananas
- blueberries
- grapes
- mangoes
- melons
- oranges
- pears
- pineapples
- raspberries
- strawberries
- tomatoes

Yes, they're fruits!

- aubergines
- broccoli
- carrots
- cauliflowers
- courgettes
- cucumbers
- green beans
- leeks
- peas
- peppers
- spinach
- sweetcorn

Here are some other fruit and veg that may be new to you. Go on – give them a try...

YAM   KOHLRABI

POMEGRANATE

PLANTAIN   RAMBUTAN

CELERIAC

More about EXERCISE

Chapter 6 was all about exercise and how **good** it is for you. If you want to be more active, but are unsure what to try first, check out this info:

1 **Find out what's on in your local area.** There will be LOADS of different classes and activities. You could try one out and see if it's for you. If not, try another.

2 **Try exercising with a friend** (perhaps the one you play computer games with, ahem!). Set targets and gradually extend them. Together, you'll motivate each other.

3 **Nobody needs to know that you're doing some exercise if you don't want them to.** Remember those ideas on page 129 you can do all on your own?

> You could save up, or ask for equipment and lessons as gifts.

4 **Some forms of exercise will cost.** You might need equipment, or to pay for a class. Bear this in mind, and research a bit first. Can you borrow any kit you need, for instance?

5 **'Exercise' really doesn't have to mean 'sport'.** It can mean juggling, rollerblading, trampolining or just walking a dog (can you borrow one, if you're dogless?). Just think 'I need to get moving', and GO FOR IT!

> Research shows that both dogs AND walking can really cheer you up. Who knew?

6 Try these 3 exercises a few times each day, building up to more as you get fitter. They will all strengthen the core muscles in your tummy:

Stomach crunches

Lie on your back with your hands crossed on your chest. Then, without straining your neck, pull in your stomach muscles and slowly lift your shoulders. Lower gradually and repeat.

Squats

Stand with your feet shoulder width apart and your arms out in front for balance. Slowly lower yourself into this position. Don't let your knees go further forward than your toes, or your bum go lower than your knees. Repeat.

Superman

Kneel down and lean forward on your arms. Stretch out one arm and the opposite leg and hold for 30 seconds. Lower your arm and leg, change sides and repeat.

7 **Finally, remember it takes time to get good at anything new.** Once you start to see results, you'll feel great. Remember, if you don't try, you'll never succeed.

Hey, we're getting quite good at this!

Take your pick

And if you are STILL stuck for ideas, here are even MORE for you. Tot up how many you've tried and then decide what you want to try next. You never know — you might be a future Tour de France winning cyclist or an Olympic rower...

- aerobics
- archery
- athletics
- badminton
- ballet
- basketball
- canoeing

- climbing
- cricket
- cycling
- dancing
- football
- gymnastics
- horse riding

- ice skating
- judo
- juggling
- karate
- rowing

- skateboarding
- tennis
- ultimate frisbee
- volleyball
- weight training

If you want to, and have the chance, try some more 'out there' activities, such as kite-boarding or sand-yachting. Visit Usborne Quicklinks (see page 4) for more exciting things to do.

Whatever gets your **body moving**, your **heart pumping** and makes you feel GOOD is ace!

Managing **STRESS**

We **ALL** worry about things from time to time, but
if you're feeling anxious <u>a lot</u> of the time, there are
some techniques you can use to help manage these
feelings. Try them out, and see which works best
for you. Even **five minutes a day** can help.

MINDFULNESS

This sounds a bit technical but
is actually incredibly simple. It involves
allowing your mind to focus on what you're doing
right now – how things sound, look, feel and smell.
In our frantic, media-obsessed world, some time
out from all the chatter is a good idea in itself.
When worries float into your mind, as they always
will, don't get caught up in them, but try instead
to return to focusing on your breathing.

Here are some ordinary, everyday
activities you could do MINDFULLY:

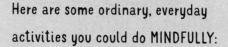

• In the shower, feel the water on
your skin, the sound it makes, how warm it is.
Breathe deeply, close your eyes and FEEL the
experience of having a shower: nothing else.

• Choose a piece of fruit you really like. How
does the skin feel, what sound does it make
when you bite into it? Eat each mouthful
slowly, thinking only about the taste and
sensations, until you finish it.

• Next time you walk anywhere, feel your feet
hit the ground with each step, listen to the
sounds around you and breathe deeply. How
does the air taste on your tongue, or feel as
it slowly fills your lungs?

WRITE IT DOWN

Writing down what's worrying you can help. As it's especially easy to worry when you're trying to fall asleep, give these ideas a go:

- Keep a notebook by your bed and jot down anything that's bothering you before you settle down. Leave your worries there for the night: you can tackle them the next day.

  - make up with Josie
  - choose title for history essay
  - visit Gran

- It helps some people to doodle their worries away, too. All you need is a sheet of paper and a pencil. Scribble your **RAGE**, loop and swirl your HAPPINESS or make up a strict, more regular pattern that helps you feel more in control of your feelings.

- If you just can't stop worrying about something, try 'taking a line for a walk'. On a sheet of paper, just let your pencil go wherever it likes. If you want to draw something specific, that's fine, but letting your pencil wander free is better.

LET IT GO

Being told to 'relax' or 'chill out' can be very annoying if you just CAN'T, but this technique (called Progressive Muscle Relaxation) can **really help.** It only takes about 10 minutes and can be done in bed before you go to sleep, sitting in a chair or even in the bath. All you need is peace and quiet. Breathe in deeply and begin...

- Breathe in deeply, clench all the muscles in your toes as tightly as you can, hold for a few seconds, then breathe out and let them go.

- Do the same with your lower leg muscles and then with your upper leg muscles.

- Slowing your breathing down even more, tense your tummy muscles and your arms and then relax each one.

- Finally – and remember that nobody's watching – screw up all the muscles in your face and neck, then let them go with one lonnnnng breath out. Ahhhhhhh.

Sit quietly, breathing slowly in and out for a few moments. Your body should feel a lot more **relaxed** than it did a few minutes ago.

WORDS TO REMEMBER

There are some key words at the heart of living healthily and you've found out about all of them in this book. Together, they make up an holistic approach to health, which means that all the different aspects of health are included. Read these words again, to remind yourself what they mean:

diet – this word has several meanings but, at its simplest, your diet is everything you eat and it includes all meals, snacks and drinks. Remember that what you eat and drink is the fuel to keep your body working well. **Chapter 3** told you how to keep an eye on your diet and make some changes, if needed, to get the balance right.

health – this word
means so much more than
'not being ill'. Your health
includes your physical,
mental and social wellbeing (how you feel with
other people). All the things you have read about
in **every chapter** of this book contribute to an
holistic view of good health. You need to look after
EVERY aspect of your health to live your best life.

food group – the five food groups are
described in **Chapter 3** of this book. Food from each
one of them forms part of a well-balanced diet, but
you should eat more of some, and less of others.
Look back again at the guide on page 48 that
showed you the proportions of each group you need
to aim for in your diet. It's important to keep that
in mind as you decide what to eat... and how much.

mental health – this aspect of your health affects how you feel, cope and react to things in life. Many people suffer from anxiety, stress, depression and loneliness, and some feel sad a lot of the time. Awful, eh? So looking after your mental health is just as important as sleeping well or eating good food: read **Chapter 8** for tips on how to cope better when things get tough.

exercise – let's call it 'being active', which sounds a lot less scary. Using your amazing body, by stretching, running, jumping, skipping, dancing – or however you choose to get moving – is so good for your health. Looking at a screen for hours really is not. Read **Chapter 6** for loads of ways of building being active into your life.

Ha! Ha! Ha!

people – yep, being with other people is good for you, but make sure you spend time with the ones that make you laugh and feel relaxed. Avoid the people that make you feel small, or make you pretend to be someone you're not. Make time for friends and family, who matter most. **Chapter 10** shows you how important other people can be.

perfectionism – do you yearn for the perfect body, flawless skin or glossy hair that blows in the breeze? And does it make you miserable if you haven't got them? If so, you may be suffering from the dreaded perfectionism, or wanting to be perfect. Social media, edited photos and an endless barrage of adverts for beauty products don't help, but **Chapter 5** looks at how to keep them in their place.